A Girl Named Rosita

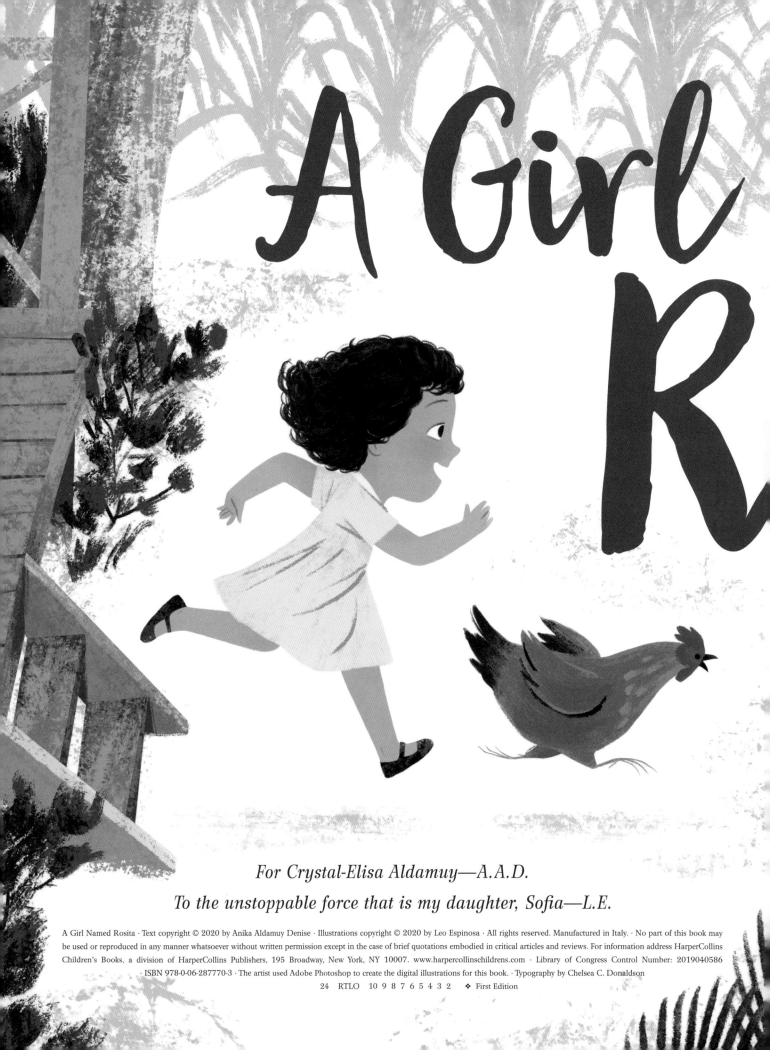

A Girl R

For Crystal-Elisa Aldamuy—A.A.D.

To the unstoppable force that is my daughter, Sofia—L.E.

A Girl Named Rosita · Text copyright © 2020 by Anika Aldamuy Denise · Illustrations copyright © 2020 by Leo Espinosa · All rights reserved. Manufactured in Italy. · No part of this book may be used or reproduced in any manner whatsoever without written permission except in the case of brief quotations embodied in critical articles and reviews. For information address HarperCollins Children's Books, a division of HarperCollins Publishers, 195 Broadway, New York, NY 10007. www.harpercollinschildrens.com · Library of Congress Control Number: 2019040586 · ISBN 978-0-06-287770-3 · The artist used Adobe Photoshop to create the digital illustrations for this book. · Typography by Chelsea C. Donaldson

24 RTLO 10 9 8 7 6 5 4 3 2 ❖ First Edition

Named osita

The Story of Rita Moreno:
Actor, Singer, Dancer,
Trailblazer!

by Anika Aldamuy Denise   *illustrated by* Leo Espinosa

HARPER
An Imprint of HarperCollinsPublishers

Juncos, Puerto Rico, 1935

In a tiny cottage tucked between El Yunque Peak and a wild fragrant rainforest lives a girl: a girl with the rhythm of the rainforest in her feet and the sweetness of the sugarcane fields in her swishing skirts.

A girl named Rosita Dolores Alverio, who loves to sing and dance for anyone who'll watch her.

step, turn, snap-kick, swish, jump, twirl!

Until early one morning, Mami whispers,
"We are moving to the mainland."
"But why isn't Francisco coming?" asks Rosita.
"He will come later," says Mami. "I am taking you first
because you are a big girl and you won't cry."

So Rosita does not cry as she waves goodbye
to her baby brother.
   In the dark, cramped cabins of the crowded
passenger ship, Rosita is quiet and brave.

After days of wobbly decks and stormy seas,
a statue of a woman wearing a crown rises up
to greet them.

"Where are the trees and flowers?"
asks Rosita.

"They will be back in summer,"
Mami explains.

That night, Rosita dreams she is back in the
tiny cottage with Francisco.

When she wakes, she does the one thing
Mami thought she wouldn't—she cries.

Rosita's new school is a fortress of brick,
where children tease her for her accent,
darker skin, and curly hair.

¡Corre! she tells herself each day on her way
home from school.
     Run! So the bullies don't catch you.
     Out of the cold and away from the noise,
she returns to a home that isn't home.

"When is Francisco coming?" Rosita asks.

"Ay, hija," says Mami. "¡Pronto, pronto!"

If she only knew more inglés, she could tell the bullies:
¡Déjenme en paz! Leave me alone!

So while Mami scrubs and scours and sweats and sews,
Rosita practices inglés in secret.

Is leaving behind her native Spanish like letting go of her native island and all the things she loves?

Fields, flowers, Francisco.

Rosita stops asking, "When is Francisco coming?" Her heart tells her he will stay in Juncos with Papi and Abuelo and she will stay in America—where she must learn to speak inglés.

Day after day, she practices until she
can speak inglés perfectly.
"I am Rosita. I am five years old."

Just as Mami promised,
the leaves return in summer,
bringing color to the concrete city—
tiny glimpses that feel like
hope.
Rosita smiles again.
And dances!

At six years old, Rosita begins dance classes.

"Paco Cansino is famous," Mami tells her. "He is the tío and teacher of Rita Hayworth, the movie star!"

Dancing the sevillanas, Rosita is a bird rising above
the rooftops, speaking a language that is all hers.
Forward, forward,
back, back, kick . . . pasada!
Right, swing, back,
side, hold . . .

Olé!

After three long years of lessons,
Paco Cansino pronounces her
ready to perform on a real stage!

The music begins.
Strum,
   strum,
      strum!
Rosita takes a breath.

clap,
clap,
clap!

Onstage, she is home.

Soon Rosita is dancing for the troops, acting on the radio,
and recording Spanish versions of hit Hollywood movies.

Why not me? thinks Rosita, seeing the studio starlets sparkle on the screen. I can be a leading lady, too.

When Rosita is sixteen, Mami marries Eddie Moreno, and Rosita decides she will take his name. .

She chooses the last name Moreno not because she loves Eddie like a father—mostly he seems like a stranger—but because it's easier for American casting directors to pronounce.

And Rosita is ready to be a star!

Then—a miracle happens.
Louis B. Mayer, the head of
MGM film studios, wants to
meet her.

Her palms are sweating as she shakes the hand of the man who can change her life.

"Sign her!" Mr. Mayer says with one look at Rosita.

Rosita Dolores Alverio Moreno is on her way to Hollywood!

In Hollywood, Rosita's name changes again.
This time, the movie studio chooses.
Ruby Fontino? Marcy Miranda? Orchid
Montenegro?
Please, she prays. Anything but Orchid!
"I've got it!" says the casting director. "How
about Rita? After Rita Hayworth!"
From that day forward, Rita Moreno she will be.

Rita Moreno is ready for Hollywood. But Hollywood isn't ready for Rita Moreno.

Years after teaching herself to speak perfect inglés, she must fake an all-purpose accent to play maidens, slaves, and Spanish spitfires: the only roles Hollywood will give to a Latina.

Some days she wants to quit. But she's come too far to give up. One day she will play an authentic character who is

bold,

proud,

strong.

In 1959, the newspapers announce
that Hollywood is making *West Side
Story*, the hit Broadway musical, into
a movie!

This film, THIS part is everything
Rita's been waiting for.

She auditions for Anita, a proud
Puerto Rican female lead.

For a month, she practices.
Step, turn, snap-kick,
        swish,
                jump,
                        TWIRL!

When the test cameras roll, she is Rosita again,
back in the concrete city.
  ¡Corre! Run! Out of the schoolyard,
past the bullies in the streets.
  Tears.
  Anger.
  Fear.
  And . . . scene.

Jaws drop at Rita's
emotional performance.
    Then—cue the music: horns,
strings, percussion!
    Step,
        turn,
            snap-kick,

swish,

jump,

twirl!

The role is hers. Rita is Anita:
bold, proud, strong.

New York City, 1962

In barrios throughout the city, Puerto Ricans gather around their television sets to watch the 34th Academy Awards.

No puertorriqueña, or any Latina, has ever won an Oscar.

A sacred silence descends.

A collective breath is held.

Who will take home the award?

"May I have the envelope, please?"

"RITA MORENO in *West Side Story*!"

"She won! She won! She did it!" her fans cry.

"I can't believe it!" says a stunned Rita, clutching her golden statue.
  With the pride of her people on her shoulders, Rosita Dolores Alverio from Juncos has made history.

Timeline

- **1950** • *So Young and So Bad* – Rita's film debut is the one and only time her name appears on a marquee as "Rosita Moreno."
- *The Toast of New Orleans* – In Rita's earliest film for MGM, she plays Tina, a Cajun girl from the Louisiana bayou, the first in a string of stereotypical ethnic roles.
- *Pagan Love Song* – Rita plays a Tahitian girl named Terru. While she is grateful for the work, in later years, Rita is openly critical of the film's flawed representation of Polynesian people and culture.

- **1952** • *Singin' in the Rain* – Rita appears alongside Gene Kelly and Debbie Reynolds in the small but memorable part of Zelda Zanders, which gains her critical acclaim and is her first studio role that isn't ethnically stereotyped.

- **1953** • Rita is let go from her contract with MGM. She makes a conscious choice to keep working, but it means signing with 20th Century Fox and playing more "dusky damsels."
- *The Yellow Tomahawk* – In this campy Western, Rita plays an indigenous woman named Honey Bear. Of all her films, Rita considers it "the worst offender" for portraying negative racial and gender stereotypes.

- **1956** • *The King and I* – For the elaborate production, Rita wears an iconic costume to play the king's slave Tuptim. While working on the film, she meets legendary choreographer Jerome Robbins, who later auditions her for *West Side Story*.

- **1961** • *West Side Story* – Rita delivers a powerhouse performance as Anita in the film adaptation of Leonard Bernstein's hit Broadway musical. On set, she is uncomfortable with makeup used to make all the Puerto Ricans the same shade of brown, yet she remains proud to be a part of the historic film.

- **1962** • Rita wins the Oscar for Best Supporting Actress for playing Anita in *West Side Story*.

- **1963** • Rita and a group of diverse celebrities attend the March on Washington, where Dr. Martin Luther King Jr. delivers his "I Have a Dream" speech, igniting Rita's lifelong dedication to political activism.

- **1961-68** • Rita boycotts film acting for seven years. Fed up with being offered demeaning roles, she refuses to play them and instead tackles stage roles in London and New York.

• **1965** • Rita marries physician Lenny Gordon at City Hall in New York City. Two years later, she becomes Mami to their daughter, Fernanda Luisa Gordon.

• **1969** • *The Night of the Following Day* – At long last, Rita returns to film, playing the lead alongside iconic movie star Marlon Brando, whom she dated for many years before marrying Lenny.

• **1971** • She joins the cast of *The Electric Company*, a children's television show, where she coins the memorable catchphrase, "Hey, you guys!" A year later, Rita wins a Grammy for the show's soundtrack.

• **1975** • For her role in Broadway's *The Ritz*, Rita wins a Tony Award. In her acceptance speech, she famously announces, "Rita Moreno is thrilled, but Rosa Dolores Alverio from Humacao, Puerto Rico, is UNDONE!"

• **1977** • Rita clinches the EGOT (Emmy, Grammy, Oscar, Tony) when her performance on *The Muppet Show*, singing alongside the wild but lovable Muppet character Animal, earns her an Emmy Award.

• **2004** • Rita receives the Presidential Medal of Freedom—the nation's highest civilian honor—from President George W. Bush.

• **2010** • President Barack Obama awards Rita the National Medal of Arts.

• **2017** • Rita captivates a new generation of fans as Lydia in Norman Lear's reboot of the classic sitcom *One Day at a Time*.

• **2019** • Peabody jurors honor Rita with a prestigious Career Achievement Award. At the ceremony, Rita dedicates the award to her mami, Rosa Maria, describing how she worked as a sweatshop seamstress to pay for rent and dance lessons so Rita could follow her dreams. "My fame is her fame. Therefore, this beautiful, precious honor is also in her honor."

• **2021** • Rita Moreno stars in Steven Spielberg's remake of *West Side Story* as Valentina, a reimagined version of Doc, the shopkeeper, in the original film.

• • •

Selected Bibliography, Articles, and Quotation Sources

"Career Achievement Award: Rita Moreno." The Peabody Awards, March 2019, www.peabodyawards.com/award-profile/career-achievement-award-rita-moreno.

Moreno, Rita. *Rita Moreno: A Memoir.* New York: Celebra, 2013.

"Rita Moreno and More Honored at Ellis Island Medal of Honor Gala." Broadway World, May 13, 2018, www.broadwayworld.com/article/Rita-Moreno-And-More-Honored-At-Ellis -Island-Medals-Of-Honor-Gala-20180513.

"Rita Moreno Reflects on Anita, Awards and Accents." *Sunday Weekend Edition*, National Public Radio, March 7, 2013.

"Rita Moreno Winning Best Supporting Actress." YouTube, Oscars, youtu.be/ZaOy0eb0Tbs.

Time. Firsts: Women Who Are Changing the World: Interviews, Photographs, Breakthroughs. New York: Time Inc. Books, 2017.

Author's Note

Rita Moreno is an actor, singer, and dancer whose career has spanned seven decades in film, television, and theater. She is one of three entertainers, and the only Latinx performer, to have earned a Peabody, Emmy, Grammy, Oscar, and Tony Award.

Born Rosa Dolores Alverio in 1931 in Humacao and raised until the age of five in Juncos, Puerto Rico, Rita's journey from daughter of rural Puerto Rican farmers to award-winning actress may seem like a fairy tale, but her path to success was paved with many sacrifices, including leaving behind loved ones—most painfully, her beloved brother Francisco when he was just a baby.

Another was having to endure Hollywood's racist and sexist attitudes—which meant accepting secondary roles rooted in gender stereotypes and riddled with cultural inaccuracies.

And yet, in the face of Hollywood's prejudices, Rita persevered. And, by doing so, inspired a generation of Latinas and other young women of color who believed they, too, could follow their dreams, thanks to the barriers she shattered and the doors she *snap-kicked–twirled* her way through.

I was one of those young women. So you can imagine my awe when I had the very unexpected opportunity to meet Rita while visiting my aunt's lake house in upstate New York. Overwhelmed (and underdressed) to meet one of my childhood idols—I froze! I had just met Rita Moreno—whose Oscar-winning role as Anita in *West Side Story* I'd played in the mirror countless times, singing "America" into my hairbrush—and I'd been too star-struck to speak! Oh, how I wished I'd found the courage to tell her that for a Puerto Rican kid from Queens who loved the performing arts, she'd been a much-needed role model and inspiration.

She still inspires me today. Not just for her groundbreaking achievements but for how she continuously uses her voice to help others. As an outspoken advocate for racial and gender equality, childhood education, immigrant families, relief for her homeland of Puerto Rico, and many other causes for which she is impassioned, Rita is a shining example of what can happen when you show up, shake things up, and give back to your community.

Upon accepting her Ellis Island Medal of Honor in 2018, Rita said this:

I do believe, with all of my heart and soul, that yearning masses will always huddle on the border of hope. And I pray that America will always be that beacon of those people's dream.

So for all that I didn't have the courage to say that unexpected afternoon by the lake, for Latinx kids who sing into their hairbrushes, for families hoping to come to America to fulfill a dream (and those fighting to stay), for women who rise up and smash ceilings—*and for Rita*—I am sharing her inspiring story.